A Crabtree Roots Book

# FARM ANIMAL FRIENDS
# LLAMAS

AMY CULLIFORD

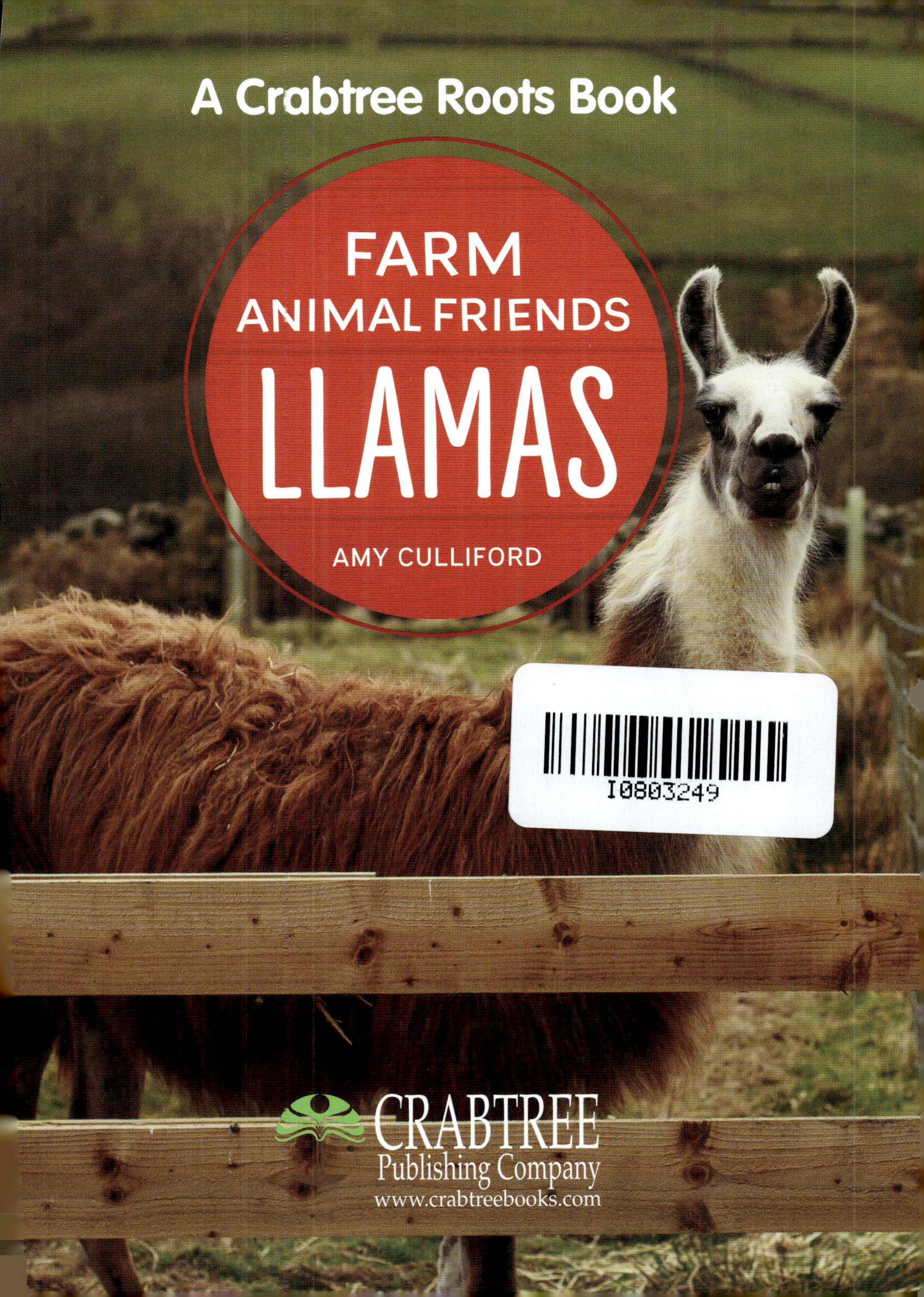



CRABTREE
Publishing Company
www.crabtreebooks.com

# School-to-Home Support for Caregivers and Teachers

This book helps children grow by letting them practice reading. Here are a few guiding questions to help the reader with building his or her comprehension skills. Possible answers appear here in red.

## Before Reading:

- What do I think this book is about?
    - *I think this book is about llamas.*
    - *I think this book is about farm animals and their friends.*
- What do I want to learn about this topic?
    - *I want to learn more about what llamas do on the farm.*
    - *I want to learn what llamas eat.*

## During Reading:

- I wonder why...
    - *I wonder why llamas have long necks.*
    - *I wonder why a llama's fur looks like wool.*
- What have I learned so far?
    - *I have learned some llamas are big and some are little.*
    - *I have learned that llamas can be brown, black, or white.*

## After Reading:

- What details did I learn about this topic?
    - *I have learned that llamas live on farms.*
    - *I have learned that llamas have wool for their coats.*
- Read the book again and look for the vocabulary words.
    - *I see the word **necks** on page 8 and the word **wool** on page 13. The other vocabulary words are found on page 14.*

This is a **llama**.

Some llamas are big, and some are little.

Llamas can be brown, black, or white.

Many llamas have long **necks**.

All llamas like to eat.

All llamas have **wool**.

# Word List

## Sight Words

a
all
and
are
be
big
black
brown
can
eat
have
is
like
little
long
many
or
some
this
to
white

## Words to Know

**llama**

**necks**

**wool**

# 33 Words

This is a **llama**.

Some llamas are big, and some are little.

Llamas can be brown, black, or white.

Many llamas have long **necks**.

All llamas like to eat.

All llamas have **wool.**

# FARM ANIMAL FRIENDS
# LLAMAS

CRABTREE Publishing Company

Written by: Amy Culliford
Designed by: Rhea Wallace
Series Development: James Earley
Proofreader: Petrice Custance
Educational Consultant: Christina Lemke M.Ed.

Photographs:
Shutterstock: Rita_Kochmarjova: cover (top left); jaromircihak: cover (top right); Lisa Stelzel: cover (bottom), p. 11; Anastasia Ponomarenko: p. 1; cbenapress: p. 3; Jeff McCollough: p. 5; fotoarte: p. 6-7; Jrs Jahangeer: p. 9; PKPhotography

Library and Archives Canada Cataloguing in Publication

CIP available at Library and Archives Canada

Library of Congress Cataloging-in-Publication Data

CIP available at Library of Congress

**Crabtree Publishing Company**

www.crabtreebooks.com 1-800-387-7650

 Printed in the U.S.A./072022/CG20220201

 In Canada: We acknowledge the financial support of the Government of Canada through the Canada Book Fund for our publishing activities.

**Published in the United States**
**Crabtree Publishing**
347 Fifth Avenue, Suite 1402-145
New York, NY, 10016

**Published in Canada**
**Crabtree Publishing**
616 Welland Ave.
St. Catharines, ON, L2M 5V6